ELIJAH'S FEATHERED FRIENDS

5 Bedtime Stories of Ravens and Miracles

BLUME POTTER

INTRODUCTION

As you tuck your children or grandchildren into bed each night, what better way to end the day than with stories that not only captivate their imaginations but also nurture their faith? Elijah's Feathered Friends: 5 Bedtime Stories of Ravens and Miracles offers a unique blend of adventure, warmth, and spiritual lessons, making it an essential addition to your bedtime story collection.

This beautifully crafted book brings to life the miraculous story of Elijah, as seen through the eyes of the humble ravens who were chosen by God to sustain him during a time of great need. Each chapter is filled with tales of trust, obedience, and divine provision—timeless themes that resonate with children and reinforce the values you hold dear.

With its engaging, witty prose and gentle life lessons, this book not only entertains but also plants seeds of faith in the hearts of young readers. As they journey with Elijah and his feathered friends, your little ones will learn about God's care and the importance of perseverance, obedience, and trust in His plan.

Whether you're a parent looking for meaningful bedtime stories or a grandparent eager to share the love of the Bible with the next generation, Elijah's Feathered Friends is the perfect way to end the day with love, laughter, and a little bit of God's wisdom.

CHAPTER ONE:
THE HUNGRY PROPHET

In the land of Israel, the sun blazed high in the sky, and the earth cracked under its relentless heat. No rain had fallen for months, and the rivers had run dry. The people and animals were thirsty and hungry, and even the trees drooped with sadness. The whole land seemed to groan under the weight of the terrible drought.

In the middle of this dry and dusty land, there was a man named Elijah. He was a prophet, chosen by God to bring messages of hope and warning to the people. But now, even Elijah was in need. His stomach growled with hunger, and his lips were parched. He had followed God's command to hide by the brook called Cherith, where he had found a small trickle of water to drink. But now, even the brook was drying up, and Elijah had nothing to eat.

As Elijah sat under a withered tree, he prayed to God for help. "O Lord," he said, "I have followed Your word, but now I am hungry and weak. Please provide for me as You have promised."

Far above, in the clear blue sky, a group of ravens soared on the wind. These birds were not known for sharing or helping others. In fact, they were scavengers, always searching for scraps to eat. But today, something strange happened. The ravens felt a gentle tug in their hearts, a divine message that was clear and strong. God was telling them to bring food to Elijah.

The ravens were confused at first. "Us? Feed a prophet?" they cawed to one another. "We are just simple birds, not providers of meals!"

But the message was clear, and the ravens knew they must obey. They flapped their wings and began to search for food. In a place where there seemed to be no food at all, they found bread and meat. With determination, the ravens grabbed the food in their beaks and flew down to where Elijah sat.

Elijah looked up in surprise as the ravens circled above him. He had never seen birds act like this before. One by one, the ravens landed near him and dropped the food at his feet. Elijah's heart filled with gratitude. He knew this was a miracle, a sign that God was watching over him.

The ravens watched as Elijah ate the bread and meat they had brought. They were still a bit puzzled by their new role as helpers, but they felt a sense of pride and peace knowing they had done something important.

As the sun began to set, Elijah bowed his head and thanked God for His provision. The ravens flew back to their nests, ready to return with more food the next day, knowing that they were part of something much bigger than themselves.

In this way, God provided for Elijah during the drought, using the most unlikely of creatures to care for His prophet. And Elijah, the hungry prophet, learned that God's provision can come in the most unexpected ways.

CHAPTER TWO:
THE MIRACLE OF BREAD

Every morning, just as the first light of dawn touched the horizon, the ravens would set out to bring food to Elijah. Among them was one raven named Rafi. Rafi was smaller than the others, with feathers as black as midnight and eyes that shone with determination. He was proud to be part of this special mission, but today was different. Today, Rafi would face challenges he had never imagined.

As Rafi swooped down to pick up the bread for Elijah, the wind suddenly picked up, whipping through the air with fierce gusts. Rafi clutched the bread tightly in his beak, but the wind pushed against him, making it hard to fly. He flapped his wings as hard as he could, fighting to stay on course.

As Rafi struggled against the wind, a hawk appeared in the sky, circling above. The hawk's sharp eyes spotted Rafi and the bread he carried. The hawk swooped down, trying to snatch the bread from Rafi's beak. Rafi darted and dodged, his heart pounding with fear. But he knew he couldn't let go of the bread. Elijah was waiting, and Rafi had a mission to complete.

Rafi flew low to the ground, weaving through the trees and bushes to escape the hawk. The hawk followed closely, its wings beating powerfully through the air. Rafi's wings were growing tired, but he pushed on, remembering why he was doing this. He was delivering God's provision to Elijah, and nothing would stop him.

Finally, after what felt like hours of flying, Rafi saw the familiar shape of Elijah sitting by the brook. With one last burst of energy, Rafi soared towards Elijah and dropped the bread at his feet. The hawk, seeing that it had lost its chance, flew away with a screech of frustration.

Elijah looked up and smiled at Rafi. He could see the little raven was tired, but also that Rafi had not given up. Elijah picked up the bread and gave thanks to God for the food and for the brave raven who had delivered it.

Rafi perched on a nearby branch, catching his breath. He felt a deep sense of satisfaction, knowing he had overcome the obstacles in his path. The wind and the hawk had tried to stop him, but Rafi had persevered. He knew that sometimes, doing what's right isn't easy, but with faith and determination, it is always possible.

That evening, as the sun dipped below the horizon, Rafi flew back to his nest, ready to rest and prepare for another day. He had learned an important lesson: when God gives you a mission, He also gives you the strength to see it through, no matter what challenges come your way.

And so, the miracle of bread continued, with the ravens faithfully bringing food to Elijah each day, showing that with perseverance and trust in God, even the smallest creatures can do great things.

CHAPTER THREE:
THE MEALTIME MESSENGERS

As the sun began to dip low in the sky, casting a golden glow over the land, the ravens knew it was time for their evening task. Each evening, they would bring meat to Elijah, just as they brought bread each morning. Among the flock was a young raven named Pip, who was new to this special mission. Pip was eager to help but still learning how to carry out his duties.

"Remember, Pip," said Rafi, the seasoned raven who had been delivering food to Elijah for some time, "this task is important. We are serving God by helping His prophet, Elijah. The meat we bring will give him the strength he needs to continue his work."

Pip nodded, determined to do his best. As the older ravens swooped down to gather pieces of meat, Pip watched carefully, trying to mimic their every move. He picked up a small piece of meat with his beak, but it felt heavy and awkward. Pip wasn't used to carrying something so large, and he wobbled in the air as he tried to fly.

The other ravens soared gracefully, each carrying their portion of meat with ease. Pip, on the other hand, struggled to keep up. He flapped his wings hard, trying to maintain his balance. The task seemed unusual and challenging for a young raven like him, but Pip knew it was important. He didn't want to let anyone down, especially not Elijah or God.

As Pip flew toward Elijah's resting place, he began to doubt himself. "What if I drop the meat?" he thought. "What if I'm not strong enough to do this?"

But then Pip remembered Rafi's words about serving God and helping others. Pip knew that obedience was about doing the right thing, even when it was difficult. He took a deep breath, steadied his wings, and focused on his mission.

When Pip finally reached Elijah, the other ravens had already delivered their meat. Pip landed gently near Elijah and carefully placed his portion at the prophet's feet. Elijah smiled warmly at the young raven, his eyes filled with gratitude.

"Thank you, little one," Elijah said, his voice kind and reassuring. "Your obedience and effort mean more than you know."

Pip felt a rush of pride and relief. He had done it! Despite the challenges and his inexperience, Pip had completed his task. As he flew back to the flock, Pip realized that serving others wasn't always easy, but it was always worthwhile. He had learned that even when a task seems unusual or difficult, obedience and a willing heart can make all the difference.

That night, as the ravens returned to their nests, Pip felt a sense of fulfillment. He knew he was part of something important, and he was grateful for the opportunity to serve. The mealtime messengers continued their faithful work, delivering meat to Elijah each evening, teaching that even the smallest acts of obedience can have a big impact.

CHAPTER FOUR:
THE VALLEY OF REST

In the quiet valley where the brook Cherith flowed, Elijah found a place of rest. The sun was warm, and the gentle sound of water trickling over stones filled the air. Each day, Elijah sat beneath the shade of a small tree, feeling the cool breeze on his face. He had no need to worry about food or drink, for the ravens brought him bread in the morning and meat in the evening, just as God had promised.

The ravens had become more than just messengers; they were Elijah's companions. As Elijah rested by the brook, the ravens would perch on nearby branches, keeping watch over him. Their dark feathers shimmered in the sunlight, and their eyes were always alert. Elijah felt a deep sense of peace knowing that God had sent these birds to care for him.

Elijah would often talk to the ravens, sharing his thoughts and prayers. Though they could not speak, the ravens seemed to understand. They would caw softly in response, as if to reassure him that everything was as it should be. Elijah knew that they were there because God had commanded them to be, and this filled his heart with gratitude.

The days passed peacefully in the valley. Elijah's strength returned, and he spent his time in prayer and reflection. He marveled at how God had provided for him in such an unexpected way. The valley, once a place of drought and desperation, had become a haven of rest and renewal.

The ravens, too, had found a sense of purpose in their daily task. Each morning and evening, they would gather their food and bring it to Elijah, knowing that they were fulfilling God's will. They no longer questioned their role but embraced it with a quiet dignity. The relationship between Elijah and the ravens was one of mutual trust and care.

As the sun set each evening, Elijah would watch the ravens fly off to their nests, their silhouettes dark against the glowing sky. He would offer a prayer of thanks for the day's provisions and for the peace that filled his heart. In the stillness of the valley, Elijah felt close to God, sustained not only by the food the ravens brought but also by the knowledge that God was with him, providing for his every need.

The valley of rest was a place of healing and peace, where Elijah learned to trust fully in God's provision. The ravens, in their faithful service, became symbols of God's care, showing that even in the hardest of times, God's peace is ever-present for those who trust in Him.

CHAPTER FIVE:
THE FINAL FLIGHT

The days in the valley of rest had been a time of peace and renewal, but as the sun rose higher each day, the brook that had sustained Elijah began to dry up. The once lively stream slowed to a trickle, and soon there was no water left. Elijah knew it was time to move on, for God had another plan for him.

The ravens sensed the change too. Each day, as they brought Elijah his food, they noticed the shrinking stream and the fading greenery. They knew their time with Elijah was coming to an end. On the morning of their final flight, the ravens gathered together, reflecting on the journey they had shared with the prophet.

"We have been part of something important," said Rafi, his voice filled with a mix of pride and sorrow. "God chose us, simple ravens, to care for His prophet. We have seen Elijah grow stronger and more peaceful because of the food we brought."

Pip, the youngest raven, who had learned so much during their mission, nodded. "At first, I didn't understand why God chose us for this task," he said. "But now I see that every role, no matter how small, is important in God's plan. We were needed, and we did our best."

The older ravens agreed. They had carried out their mission faithfully, and now they felt a sense of fulfillment. Though their time with Elijah was ending, they knew that they had played a crucial part in his journey. They had been more than just birds; they had been God's messengers, bringing hope and sustenance to a weary soul.

As Elijah prepared to leave the valley, he looked up at the ravens one last time. "Thank you, my friends," he said with a gentle smile. "You have been faithful, and your service will not be forgotten."

The ravens took to the sky, their wings beating in unison as they made their final flight over the valley. They felt a deep sense of peace, knowing that they had completed their mission. As they soared higher, they knew that their role in God's work had been important, and they were grateful for the opportunity to serve.

Elijah watched the ravens disappear into the distance, his heart full of gratitude. He knew that God's provision had come in many forms, and the ravens had been a vital part of that provision. As he turned to leave the valley, Elijah carried with him the lessons of faithfulness and trust that the ravens had shown him.

The story of the ravens and Elijah is a reminder that every role, no matter how small, is important in God's work. The ravens had fulfilled their purpose with faithfulness, and their journey was a testament to the power of obedience and the significance of even the simplest acts in God's grand plan.